New Yeats Papers XVI
General Editor: Liam Miller

W. B. Yeats *and* James Stephens.
Medallion portraits by T. Spicer-Simpson.

Richard J. Finneran

The Olympian
& the Leprechaun

W. B. Yeats and James Stephens

The Dolmen Press Dublin

New Yeats Papers XVI

Set in Pilgrim type with Perpetua display
and printed and published in the Republic of Ireland
at the Dolmen Press
North Richmond Industrial Estate, North Richmond Street, Dublin 1

First published 1978

ISBN 0 85105 338 6

Distributed in the United States of America and in Canada by
Humanities Press Inc.
171 First Avenue, Atlantic Highlands, N.J. 07716

Contents

The Olympian and the Leprechaun:
W. B. Yeats and James Stephens

Frontispiece

Portrait-medallions of Stephens (1913) and Yeats (1922) by Theodore Spicer-Simson; reproduced in his *Men of Letters of the British Isles* (1924). Stephens helped Spicer-Simson gain an introduction to Yeats (*LJS* 277). Yeats recorded his opinion of his medallion in 'Ireland, 1921–1931' (*Spectator*, 30 January 1932): 'When I reached home I took from the mantelpiece a bronze medal of myself and studied the little shamrock the American medallist had put after the date. But there had been no transformation; the disgust that will always keep me from printing that portrait in any book of mine, or forgiving its creator, had increased, as though the ascent of the other symbols had left the shamrock the more alone with its associations of drink and jocularity' (*Uncollected Prose*, II, 486–87).

General Editor: Liam Miller

to Mary

The Olympian and the Leprechaun :
W. B. Yeats and James Stephens[1]

One might begin by recalling the evening of Friday, 20 November 1914, in Dublin. The Gaelic Society of Trinity College, having been prohibited by the then Vice-Provost John Pentland Mahaffy from holding their Thomas Davis Centenary meeting within college grounds because one of the announced speakers was 'a man called Pearse' (Padraic H. Pearse, executed less than two years later for his considerable part in the Easter Rebellion), has deferred to the Students' National Literary Society; an expanded version of the planned meeting is being held in the Antient Concert Rooms. One of the speakers is the acknowledged leader of the Irish Literary Renaissance, W. B. Yeats, whose *The Countess Cathleen* had been performed in the same hall some fifteen years earlier. After tracing his ambivalent feelings towards Davis — arguing that he had 'moral quality' but was not a good writer — Yeats concludes his speech with a prophecy :

When the other day I read *The Demigods* of Mr. James Stephens, I felt that he alone by himself — and he has the Abbey Players to help him, the early lyrics of Æ and much else — could take care of the future of Irish literature, till the next reaction comes.[2]

Yeats did not give such fulsome praise often, least of all in public forums; and so his prediction, though regrettably unfulfilled, demands our attention. As several generations of Yeats scholars have taught us, the best place to look for further information on a reference in Yeats is usually elsewhere in his own writings. But with the question of his attitudes towards Stephens that methodology fails to produce significant results : a handful of references in some essays and autobiographical pieces, scarcely more in the various collections of correspondence now available. However, when these scattered allusions are combined with those by Stephens and with Yeats's unpublished letters, the contours of the relationship can be traced.

I : 1909–1914

I conjecture that Yeats and Stephens first met on 25 April 1909, at one of Æ's Sunday evenings. Although Stephens had published an isolated short story in 1905, he had begun to acquire a literary reputation in the spring of 1907 with regular appearances in the pages of Arthur Griffith's *Sinn Féin* (beginning on 20 April). At this time relations between Æ and Yeats were hostile, caused in the main by their differences over the policies of the Abbey Theatre in

1904–05.[3] And if George Moore's account in *Vale* (1914) is trust-
worthy, Æ was in search of a disciple to match — or top — Yeats's
discovery of Synge. Moore begins by recalling a conversation with
Yeats:

> You don't think that Æ will ever discover any one in *Sinn Féin* comparable
> to Synge?
> Yeats threw up his hands.
> It would be better, he said, if all his little folk went back to their desks.

When this conversation is reported to Æ, he vows 'So Willie says
that I shall never find anything that will compare with Synge. Well,
we shall see.'

> And every Thursday evening the columns of *Sinn Féin* were searched, and
> every lilt considered, and every accent noted; but the days and the weeks
> went by without a new peep-o-peep, sweet, sweet, until the day that James
> Stephens began to trill; and recognising at once a new songster, Æ put on his
> hat and went away with his cage, discovering him in a lawyer's office. A
> great head and two soft brown eyes looked at him over a typewriter, and an
> alert and intelligent voice asked him whom he wanted to see. Æ said that he
> was looking for James Stephens, a poet, and the typist answered: I am he.[4]

The date would have been 27 June 1907, the poem 'Nature ag
Labhairt' (Nature Speaking', *Sinn Féin*, 29 June 1907).

   Since Stephens was immediately admitted into Æ's literary circle,
it is possible that he met Yeats in the autumn of 1907, when
the latter returned from Coole Park. If so, or if they met at any
time before April 1909, no record survives. The main evidence
which might suggest an earlier meeting is the publication of two of
Stephens's poems as Cuala Press Broadsides ('Where the Demons
Grin', November 1908; 'Why Tomas Cam Was Grumpy', January
1909). But Yeats himself, often being away from Dublin, seems to
have had little involvement with the Broadsides, the guiding force
behind which was his brother, Jack B. Yeats.[5] And Æ, who had been
appointed to an Advisory Committee for the Cuala (then Dun Emer)
Press on 29 September 1904, certainly would have recommended
the publication of Stephens's poems.[6]

   Thus I believe that the first meeting between the two writers is
the occasion mentioned in an entry in Yeats's Journal on Tuesday,
27 April 1909:

> Went to Russell's Sunday night — everybody either too tall or too short, or
> crooked or lop-sided. One woman had that terrible thing in a woman, an
> excited voice, and an intellect without self-possession. There was a bad poet
> with a swollen neck.[7]

Stephens was approximately five feet tall (four feet, ten inches, according to some accounts); and, as Oliver St. John Gogarty more nicely phrases it in the *DNB* (1941–50), he had a 'full throat, due to a goitre.' Further, just before this entry in his Journal Yeats had written a draft of 'To a Poet, Who Would Have Me Praise Certain Bad Poets, Imitators of His and Mine', which almost surely refers in part to Stephens.[8] But the most telling piece of evidence for the identity of the 'bad poet with a swollen neck' is Yeats's note to that sentence, added at some later date : 'No, an excellent poet; I did not know his good work then.'[9]

George Moore's account of the first meeting between Yeats and Stephens confirms the original entry in the Journal :

> Yeats was the blindest of us all, and it was with ill grace that he consented to hear Æ read the poems, giving his opinion casually; and when Æ spoke of the advantage the publication of a volume would be to Stephens, he answered: For me, the aesthetical question : for you, my dear friend, the philanthropic.[10]

With these remarks in mind, we can be relatively confident about the nature of Yeats's reply when, as he explained in a letter to Lady Gregory on 25 November 1909, 'at dinner the Prime Minister began by questioning me about Stephen's [*sic*] poetry which he had been reading'[11] — unless, that is, Yeats allowed the patriotic question to take precedence over the 'aesthetical'.

For almost the next three years there seems to have been little or no contact between Stephens and Yeats, the latter being, as he later noted, 'not friendly' with Æ's 'centre'.[12] The start of a significant relationship dates from 2 May 1912, when the 'Present-Day Criticism' column of A. R. Orage's *The New Age* carried 'a short review, by request, of that affecting tragedy, "The Land of Heart's Desire", by Mr. William Butler Yeats.' This unsigned commentary on the 1912 revision of the play was neither short nor fair-minded, consisting primarily of a hostile plot summary and gratuitous comparisons with Addison, Dryden, Milton, Keats, and Shakespeare. 'We can make nothing whatever of these mystifications,' the reviewer wrote, which 'are all as sacredly obscure to us as he [Yeats] could wish them to be.' Finding Yeats's style 'uncouth', the commentator concluded that 'we find it difficult to be serious about this vague, pale, gaping drama' and that Yeats 'is one of the many revenges Ireland has taken upon us.'[13]

Stephens refused to let this pass, and he responded with a lengthy letter published in the next issue (9 May). Accusing the *New Age* writer 'of making no reasonable effort to critically examine Mr.

Yeats's poem', Stephens objected to the touchstone method of comparative passages and concluded that

There are, indeed, in this age many writers who are bad, treacherous artists, unfitted for anything but reprobation : but the number of those precious writers who may be praised is too small to be further curtailed by you, and of these Mr. Yeats is one.[14]

Yeats communicated his gratitude to Stephens in an unpublished letter of 11 May [1912] from London. Noting that he had received an unusually deferential treatment from some people in his local paper shop, Yeats explained that 'Presently one of them said "We have just been reading an article on you in the New Age, Sir". Thereupon I bought the New Age & found your most eloquent letter, for which I thank you very much.' Yeats went on to say that Seumas O'Sullivan's *Poems* (1912) and Stephens's *The Hill of Vision* (1912)

have been on the table beside my chair, when not in my hand, all this week, & have been a great pleasure to me. I found something of William Blake in your "Old, Old Man"[.] "Wind and Tree" is perfectly said & perfectly thought & that is but to say that it uses live ["life" cancelled]; but there are many fine things.

Yeats was clearly correct in seeing the influence of Blake on 'Said the Old-Old Man to the Young-Young Man', which reads in part :

> The lips of desire smile to hide
> The teeth of fierce oppression inside.
> The hand that gives and gives alway
> Only waits a time to slay.
> The eyes that woo with a fiery stare
> Are the eyes that roam anywhere.
> The kiss that is quick, and mad, and sweet
> Rolls the gutters along the street.[15]

'Wind and Tree', which also has echoes of Blake, was to remain one of Yeats's favourite Stephens poems.

Stephens surely replied to Yeats, but apparently his letter has not survived. We do have, however, a letter from Yeats to Lady Gregory in May 1912 in which he compares O'Sullivan (the pen name of James Sullivan Starkey) and Stephens. His judgement here on Stephens is somewhat less laudatory but nevertheless affirmative.

I have been reading James Stephens' poems and Starkie's. I think that Stephens has very fine lines and verses, but is a good deal spoiled by his schoolboy theology of defiance, but at his best he really is very fine. Starkie, on the other hand, has surprised me with his really delicate technical skill, he has gradually shaped himself into real force and beauty. He is a good deal better than Stephens, but Stephens is younger.[16]

At about this same time, the anonymous writer of the Yeats review published in *The New Age* for 16 May 1912 a rejoinder defending himself and attacking Stephens. Well versed in the wars of journalism, Yeats wrote on 19 May [1912] to admonish Stephens: 'Dont waste your time on him [—] he does not write well enough to matter.' He added that

it has given me great pleasure that you have defended me, not because his attack was any different from dozen of others these twenty years — "Fleet Street" can never like either you or me for we are free men and they bound — but because one is not often defended from Ireland & still more because you are yourself.

Yeats then apologized that he had been dilatory in responding to Stephens's achievement: 'I had only seen your poetry in quotation until very lately, (inexcusable of me I admit), & now I know little of our time that excites me more than that stanza which contains the line "The sea shall tramp with banners on the shore".' Yeats here refers to a section of 'To the Tree', a poem which shows the influence not so much of Blake as of Shelley:

> Rapture and joy and ecstasy and pain!
> The windy trumpets of the void shall soar
> Over the sky. The Morning Stars again
> Will sing together joyous as of yore:
> The sea shall tramp with banners on the shore:
> The little hills skip merrily along
>
> The forest leave its field and with a roar
> Stride down the pathway shouting out a song,
> And everything be happy as the day is long.[17]

In his reply (now lost) to Yeats's praise, Stephens must have asked for some more detailed criticism of his poetry. Yeats wrote on 31 May 1912 that he had taken 'your poems with me into the country & I have been reading them to two friends, lovers of poetry.' Their verdict was that the Shelleyean conclusion to 'A Prelude and A Song' 'is perhaps the most beautiful thing in the book.' (Yeats added 'I had picked it out before I got your letter.') Yeats then continued with his personal judgment of Stephens's talent:

I like you always best when you are trying to create beauty. In fact I should have found out long ago how much I admire your work if your reviewers had not insisted upon quoting nothing but your high spirits. . . .
Everyone, except those who really love poetry, will tell you that you are at your best in poems like "Nora Criona" & almost every reviewer will prefer them, because they give their secret to a man in a hurry. I myself always feel one should distrust any work of one's own which impresses people as "Strong" — it means one is giving them the logs instead of the fire.

'Nora Criona' is clearly indebted to Browning, the third of the major influences on Stephens's early poetry; so in sum, Yeats was encouraging the Blakean and Shelleyean echoes in Stephens while objecting to those of Browning. I suggest, then, that Yeats saw in the Stephens of *The Hill of Vision* a poet overly derivative — still 'digest[ing] his ancestors' (*LJS* 176), as Stephens would put it — but one at least derivative of the right people and with a strong sense of craft and the potential for growth.

Thus the next several years witnessed the most frequent contact between Yeats and Stephens. For instance, in the spring of 1913 they were both studying French[18] and, if Stephen MacKenna's memory is correct, joined forces with little success:

Jamesy Stephens and W. B. Yeats once hired a Frenchman to teach them French together: he began with a quarter of an hour on the rules for the agreement of the past participles: Jamesy at last broke in: "Excuse me, M. Dupont, what is meant by the agreement of the past participle?" and W.B. said, "I was just going to ask you Monnshure, what is a past participle?"[19]

In March of this year a celebration of some sort was arranged for Stephens in Dublin (probably a farewell dinner, as Stephens had doubtless announced his intention to move to Paris in May 1913). Yeats wrote to Mrs. Ellen Duncan of the Municipal Gallery of Modern Art to apologize for not being able to attend and to ask the Chairman 'to say that I have written my deep regret at not being able to be in Dublin to do honour to the author of "The Prelude and a song"[,] one of the most beautiful poems of our time.' As to Stephens's attitudes towards Yeats in this period, although to some friends he would express his 'intimate conviction that Æ is a greater poet than Yeats' (*LJS* 80), he would more often admit that Yeats was the only 'first class poet in the world' (*LJS* 52).

In the autumn of 1913 Yeats was one of a committee of six charged with awarding the Polignac Prize, a grant of £100 made by the Academic Committee of the Royal Society of Literature. Intended to encourage the work of younger writers, the previous awards had gone to Walter de la Mare in 1911 and to John Masefield in 1912. For the 1913 prize Yeats proposed Stephens on the basis of *The Crock of Gold* (1912), and his suggestion won the approval of the committee. Yeats wrote to Stephens from Coole Park on 18 October 1913:

I write to give you what I hope is a pleasant piece of news. You will receive in a few days a notification from the Academic Committee that you have been awarded the Polignac prize, which is £100, for the Crock of Gold, which we consider the best book by a young writer published last year. You will I think be expected to come to London to receive it on Nov 28. I, as the proposer of the award speak the eulogy upon your book. You will meet a great many distinguished people, though I think the meeting will rather bore you. . . . The prize is a real distinction.

Stephens later recalled (*LJS* 118) that he had to borrow the money for the fare from Paris to London, but he was present in the Caxton Hall to hear Yeats's speech. Although he described the ceremony as a 'horrid ordeal' (*LJS* 110), he must have been pleased to hear Yeats state that 'Mr. Stephens has made an extravagant language, an extravagant world which enables him to speak and to symbolize his emotions and hidden thoughts, almost as fully as if he were an Elizabethan dramatist with the mediaeval gag but just taken out of his mouth.' Yeats saw in Stephens 'proof that my native city has begun to live with a deeper life.' He praised Stephens's ability to adopt legendary and folkloric material — as he had long argued Irish writers must do — and also noted that 'Mr. Stephens had perhaps deserved our award for certain of his poems.' From his understanding of Blake and from his knowledge of Irish matter, in short, Stephens has been able to create a 'phantasmagoria of eloquent people' who express what 'the rest of us are longing to say but are compelled to keep hidden within us.' [20]

Having praised Stephens in England, Yeats lost no time in accomplishing the same thing in America. Shortly after he arrived there on a lecture tour, he told an interviewer for the *New York Times* that

For a long time Ireland produced nothing but plays, but during the last few years we have had James Stephens's "Crock of Gold," a beautiful[,] fantastic story of Irish life and wild humor. It is the latest literary event in Ireland, and it is a great comfort to me that Stephens is giving us the other side of Irish life. He is not a popular novelist, but he is trying to write the finest literature.[21]

Doubtless at his son's urging, John Butler Yeats began to take an interest in Stephens. On 10 May 1914 he wrote his son from New York, commenting at length on Stephens's 'An Essay in Cubes' (*English Review*, April 1914). J. B. Yeats was uncertain about Stephens's abilities:

Whether Stephens is a poet or a prose writer turns upon whether or not he is enough self-centered to do his thinking and his feeling all by himself. If he cannot do his best without having someone to assail or cajole or persuade then he is one of the prose writers — and only incidentally a poet. The true poet is all the time a visionary and whether with friends or not, as much alone as a man on his death bed.[22]

The day after his father wrote this letter, Yeats arrived in Mirebeau, France, in the company of Maud Gonne and Everard Feilding, to investigate an alleged miracle.[23] Yeats spent some time in Paris before returning to London and visited Stephens (probably with Maud Gonne, a mutual friend; trivia experts may like to know that the Minnaloushe of 'The Cat and the Moon' was given to Maud by Stephens). Stephens described these visits in a letter to Thomas Bodkin on 11 July 1914:

> Yeats was over here a few weeks ago — he dined a couple of times with us & I find that he more than improves on acquaintence. He was really modest & he listened with quietude to a few of my poems & spoke of them afterwards as though he had been interested. Perhaps he was'nt, yet it was tres gentille of him n'est pas? (*LJS* 138)

We can now understand the background to Yeats's conclusion to his Thomas Davis address the following autumn. By stating that Stephens 'could take care of the future of Irish literature', Yeats was affirming an opinion he had held since the spring of 1912. Indeed, the reference to *The Demi-Gods* suggests that Yeats was following Stephens's career closely, as the novel had been published only a month before the Davis meeting (14 October 1914). Yeats sent his copy of the novel to Lady Gregory, who came to share his evaluation of Stephens's talent. She wrote to Yeats in 1915 that 'I return Stephens' book. I don't care much for the inset stories, but otherwise I think it is a very fine book — infinitely better than Anatole France's (*Le Retour des Dieux*) which is thin and an echo — this is original and has a background. . . .'[24]

Yeats's most detailed commentary on *The Demi-Gods* is contained in a letter to Stephens on 31 January [1915] from Stone Cottage. After apologizing for the delay in sending his comments, Yeats wrote:

> I think the book most beautiful and wise, and a great technical advance on the "Crock of Gold." It is all of a piece, whereas "The Crock of Gold" was made up of separated elements. The tinker, the girl and the donkey are always delightful, and your masterpiece about the threepenny bit is the better for the new setting.[25] The man thrashed by his higher self is an exhillerating person. There is only one criticism. I don't like the very theosophical story about the man who at some astronomical period in the past, lacks a sense of humour. I think you ought to try and rewrite that story, leaving out all definitely theosophical terms.

Yeats also noted that he had heard the book praised by many people, including Mabel Beardsley and Charles Ricketts. Little wonder that in August 1915 Yeats told Edmund Gosse that James Joyce 'and James Stephens are the most promising people we have in Ireland.'[26]

II : 1915–1938

I have suggested elsewhere that Yeats's comments on Stephens in the first years of their friendship — particularly those in the public speeches of 1913 and 1914 — were instrumental in Stephens's decision to return from Paris to Dublin and to undertake a large-scale project which would certify his position in Anglo-Irish literature.[27] Return he did, in August 1915, but his plans were not to be fulfilled. And although the two writers remained in contact, after 1915 or so their relationship clearly decreased in intensity and importance.

Several meetings during the next few years can be documented. On 6 July 1917 Stephens witnessed a reading of Yeats's *The Dreaming of the Bones* in the home of Gogarty. He wrote to his host the next day that although the drama was 'marvellous', he disliked the 'artifice' of the Noh form : 'The drum, that is, & the unwinding cloth, & the little journeys round the stage. The play is so beautiful that these first aids to the feeble are not needed. . . .' (*LJS* 219). A few days later Yeats described his Dublin visit to Olivia Shakespear : 'Stevens [?Stephens] and Russell and Hyde all called to see me and I lived in a whirl of excellent talk.' [28] In October of this year Stephens felt intimate enough about Yeats's feelings to humorously write to an American professor about the 'secret' behind his marriage :

Yeats wants to do everything that is in the tradition and is prepared at a moments notice to be a martyr to art. The chiefs of the craft have all written an Epithalamium . . . Yeats must do as has been done, and he is unable to enter into the miseries of his friends sufficiently deeply to do an epithalamium for them; therefore, he seeks the immediate personal contact, and if, at his age, there is an epithalamium in reach he will hook it down and print it in his next volume. The poor man will then wonder why the girl doesnt go home. (*LJS* 233)

In April of 1918 Stephens had the opportunity to meet Mrs. Yeats, receiving an invitation from the Yeatses for dinner at the Gresham Hotel.[29] A month later, on 17 May, Yeats and Stephens joined with Lady Gregory, Æ, and Douglas Hyde in a letter to the press protesting against English conscription in Ireland : 'We . . . feel compelled to appeal and protest against the enforcement of conscription in our country, believing, as we do, that such action will destroy all hope of peace in Ireland and goodwill towards England in our lifetime.' [30] Late in 1918 he joined with Yeats and others in founding the Dublin Drama League; Yeats was President, Stephens Vice-President.[31] Early in 1919 Yeats happily informed Lady Gregory that 'James Stephens is the first disciple of "The System",' referring to his work on what would become *A Vision* (1926).[32] (Stephens's interest in that work, though, was short-lived and doubtless less than fully comprehending.[33])

In April of 1919 Yeats was present at a gathering in Stephens's home and heard him read two of the selections from the forthcoming *Irish Fairy Tales* (1920).[34] In America the following year, Yeats recalled that work when he discussed Irish literature with an interviewer. He linked Stephens with Lady Gregory, Synge, and Lord Dunsany as 'all solitaries . . . and not one of them ever modified a line or a word for the sake of the crowd'. Moreover,

James Stephens is by far the biggest literary man in Dublin. . . . Everybody should know his "Crock of Gold" and "Mary, Mary" and his latest book of verses, "Reincarnations", in which his best poems can be found. His prose style is very beautiful. He is at work now on what will probably be his finest book, a collection of fragments of old Irish legends in prose, like an Irish Arabian Nights.[35]

Yeats also referred to *Reincarnations* in *The Trembling of the Veil* (1922), where he mis-quotes two lines from 'Egan O'Rahilly', describes the poem as 'a translation from the Gaelic that is itself a masterpiece of concentrated passion', but does not name the author.[36]

For his part, the younger writer was using the pages of *The Dial* to publish his public comments on Yeats. In his 'Irish Letter' (June 1924), for instance, Stephens pointed to Yeats as representative of 'Irish' poetry and provided evidence from two early lyrics, 'The Lover Speaks to the Hearers of his Songs in Coming Days' and 'The Withering of the Boughs' (*LJS* 305). In his 'Dublin Letter' (August 1924), Stephens noted in passing that 'Ireland has used Mr Yeats to write her lyrics, but she adopted the gentle poet with a certain formalism, as of one who should lament kings only and should make love only to a queen' (*LJS* 314).

The next certain meeting between Yeats and Stephens occurred at the *Aonach Tailteann* festival in Dublin in August 1924, at which Stephens's *Deirdre* (1923) was awarded the prize for the best work of fiction in the last three years and Yeats presented the medal. Stephens wrote his wife that 'Gogarty and Yeats are in their glory, & Yeats has bought a tall hat' (*LJS* 316).

After Stephens moved to London in January 1925, contact with Yeats naturally diminished. In December 1925, though, Yeats still suggested Stephens for membership on a three-man 'committee of publication' to 'make possible a modern Gaelic literature', noting that Stephens 'is always working at his Irish.' [37] But the absence of any intimate friendship can be seen in the fact that it was Sir

Frederick Macmillan, and not Yeats, who sent Stephens a copy of Yeats's *Autobiographies* (1926). Stephens wrote to their mutual publisher that 'I have already dipped into it, & find it everywhere excellent' (*LJS* 353) — a comment at odds with his annotation, which notes that 'In this book Yeats is only earnest when speaking of Johnson, & Symons & Dowson etc.' [38]

When Yeats first conceived of an Irish Academy of Letters in 1926, Stephens was on his list of the ten proposed members; when the Academy eventually came into being in 1932, Stephens was still one of the twenty 'Founder Members'. [39] In his 1930 diary Yeats remarked that 'James Stephens has read the Tain in the light of the Veda but the time is against him and he is silent', referring to the fact that only two of the projected five volumes of Stephens's redaction of the Táin had been published, and none since 1924; but he also went on to link Synge's work with 'James Stephens's strange exciting figures' as indications that 'We are casting off crown and mitre that we may lay our heads on mother earth.' [40]

One of the two volumes of the Táin saga which did appear has an important place in the history of the Yeats/Stephens relationship: *In the Land of Youth* (1924). It is uncertain just when Yeats read the novel, but it was no later than 2 December 1930, when he told Olivia Shakespear that 'James Stephens's three best books are The Demigods — it came out at the same time as Anatole France's book about the angels and has the same theme — I prefer it, The Crock of Gold and The Land of Youth, both of which I have loved.' [41] So it would have been between 1927 and 1931 that Yeats made the following comment in one of the typescripts of the revised version of *A Vision* (1937):

A year ago I read James Stephens' "Land of Yotuh" [*sic*] and felt that he had created an image of Ireland that is so ancient and so modern that it must be true. There was no philosophy, nothing but instinct, and yet I felt that philosophy had gone to the making of it, that he had been able to add something that had fallen out of the legends during the intervening Christian centuries. When I spoke to him about it he gave me a little book of "The Thirteen principal Upanishads" that I have studied, as the first paragraphs of my Fourth Book attest as well as my ignorance permitted. [42]

Corroboration for this borrowing is found in a letter from Stephens to Yeats on 26 July 1935, in which he notes Yeats's essay in the July issue of *The Criterion* with the following remark: 'I saw an essay by you today on the Manduka Upanishad. I think I lent that to you years ago. Tis a wonderful Upanishad. My copy had the

Guadapada and Shankara commentaries' (*LJS* 388). My guess is that the book in question was *The Mândûkyopanishad, with Guadapâda's Kârikâs and the Bhâshya of S'ankara*, trans. Manilal N. Dvivedi (1894).[43] But regardless of the particular edition, Stephens can claim partial credit for introducing Yeats to the Upanishads — an event which clearly had an important effect on his thought and which also issued in *The Ten Principal Upanishads* (1937) by Yeats and Shree Purohit Swami — the single volume in Stephens's library with an inscription by Yeats.

Yeats's admiration for *In the Land of Youth* explains, I think, why in the 1930's he added Stephens's name to some of his famous and select lists of important writers. In the introduction to *Fighting the Waves* in 1932, for example, Yeats explained that 'Lady Gregory, John Synge and I, Standish O'Grady before us, James Stephens after us, planned a literature, comic or tragic, founded upon the inventions and habits of Gaelic-speaking Ireland.'[44] He told the audiences on his 1932–33 lecture tour in America that 'Lady Gregory, John Synge and I, and James Stephens, who came somewhat later, are the typical figures of the first movement of thought after the death of Parnell.'[45] Finally, probably remembering the rivalry between Æ and himself when he first met Stephens and the contest for 'disciples' noted by George Moore in *Vale*, Yeats laid to rest the old tensions in his 11 October 1936 broadcast on 'Modern Poetry': 'Instead of turning to impersonal philosophy, they [Irish poets] have hardened and deepened their personalities. I could have taken as examples Synge or James Stephens, men I have never ceased to delight in.'[46]

However, Yeats's interest in Stephens's work was not confined to his fiction. Writing to him on 26 September [1932] about the Irish Academy of Letters, Yeats explained that 'a substantial part of my inagural lecture at "the Peacock Theatre" dealt with you & your poets [*sic*]. I read out two of your poems.'[47] Thus Stephens's poems were to find a place in both the new series of *Broadsides* and the *Oxford Book of Modern Verse* (1936). Included in the Broadsides were 'The Fifteen Acres' (August 1935), 'The Main-Deep' (April 1937), and 'The Rivals' (June 1937). The latter two form part of the selection of eight in the *Oxford Book of Modern Verse*: three from *Songs from the Clay* (1915), four from *Reincarnations* (1918), and one from *A Poetry Recital* (1925); surprisingly none of the poems from *The Hill of Vision* which Yeats had once so admired.[48] In the Introduction Yeats expresses his regret that 'I have been able to say but little of translations and interpretations of modern and medieval Gaelic literature by Lady Gregory, James Stephens, Frank

O'Connor'; but he does quote a portion of 'Egan O'Rahilly' as evidence that Stephens had helped to make the older Gaelic poets 'symbols of our pride'. More importantly, in the very brief discussion of his own work Yeats explains that at times he has been 'of the same school with John Synge and James Stephens'.[50]

At the same time Stephens was also involved in an editorial project — an unpublished anthology of writings by members of the Irish Academy of Letters — and this is the subject of the only extant exchange of correspondence between Stephens and Yeats. Stephens wrote on 26 July 1935 to remind Yeats that he had not yet submitted his contribution, in the same letter praising his late plays as the first example of 'pure drama' (*LJS* 388). Yeats replied on 25 September, suggesting that Stephens's co-editor should 'write a letter [to] the secretary of the Academy'; apparently Yeats thought that Stephens had requested a blanket permission to publish works by the members. Yeats wrote again on 5 October 1935, explaining that since he had not heard from Stephens he raised the question himself with the Academy: 'The Academy gives you its blessing and permits you to use its name, but says that you must deal with the individual members. I dont think you will meet any difficulty; everybody is friendly and considers the book a good advertisement.' After offering to waive any fee for his own work, but not making a selection as Stephens had requested, Yeats ended as follows:

Now another matter; we want you to act with O'Sullivan and myself as the judges awarding the Casement prize which this time goes to verse. The book may be any book of verse by an Irishman published during the two years ending January 1935. I cant think of any book except Higgins' "Arable Holdings"[.] Can you?

Apparently Stephens could not, as the Cuala Press volume won the award.

During the 1930's Yeats and Stephens also had a mutual interest in the speaking of verse and in radio broadcasting. Yeats had included some of Stephens's poems in his broadcast on 1 February 1937 on Radio Eireann.[51] In the same year, according to Joseph Hone, 'Yeats also proposed a broadcast debate between himself and James Stephens' on the following topics:

That it is not the duty of the artist to paint beautiful women and beautiful places is nonsense. That the exclusion of sex appeal from poetry, painting and sculpture is nonsense (are the films alone to impose their ideas upon the sexual instinct?). That, on the contrary, all arts are an expression of desire — exciting desirable life, exalting desirable death. That all arts must be united again, painting and literature, poetry and music. Bless synthesis; damn Whistler and his five o'clock.[52]

I think this proposal was made in late March 1937, as among the Stephens Papers is a telegram from Yeats inviting him to dinner at the Athenæum Club on either 28 or 29 March. Stephens may have dined with Yeats, but he declined to join the proposed debating society. (Edmund Dulac took his place, but the debate was never held.)

There are two final references to Stephens in Yeats's works, one certain, the other probable. In the 1937 'General Introduction for my Work', an essay which Yeats intended as the first item in his *Collected Works*, he includes Stephens in a select list of five. Referring to the eclectic nature of Irish thought, Yeats remarks 'That tapestry filled the scene at the birth of modern Irish literature, it is there in the Synge of *The Well of the Saints*, in James Stephens, and in Lady Gregory throughout, in all of George Russell that did not come from the Upanishads, and in all but my later poetry.'[53] A few months later, in July 1938, Yeats was writing 'The Man and the Echo', which concludes

> A stricken rabbit in crying out,
> And its cry distracts my thought.[54]

Jon Stallworthy has suggested that in these lines 'there is also a resemblance, probably no more than coincidental, to James Stephens's best-known poem, "The Snare". . . .'[55] 'The Snare' begins

> I hear a sudden cry of pain!
> There is a rabbit in a snare :
> Now I hear the cry again,
> But I cannot tell from where.

The poem concludes with the speaker still 'searching everywhere' for the rabbit.[56] Considering Yeats's interest in Stephens which we have traced, and also that in the Stephens volume from which Yeats made his *Oxford Book of Modern Verse* selection 'The Snare' is but two pages removed from one of the poems he chose, I suggest that Stallworthy's 'probably no more than coincidental' might more justly read 'probably intentional'. If so, it is a subtle tribute by the dying poet to his friend of almost thirty years.

III: 1939–1948

For Yeats, of course, the rest is silence. Stephens, however, was to live for over a decade after Yeats's death and to comment extensively on his work. In a review of another anthology a few months after Yeats died, for instance, he described the *Oxford Book of Modern*

Verse as 'possibly the worst anthology in English', adding that Yeats 'believed that other poets were pretty bad, and, by a self-preserving instinct, he chose their pretty-bad stuff for his anthology.' [57] But more typical of his attitude is a 1940 review of the memorial volume *Scattering Branches*, in which Stephens states that he 'had always mistrusted his prose' but pays tribute to Yeats's achievements as a poet, dramatist, and critic. [58]

The bulk of Stephens's retrospective commentary on Yeats was made in various B.B.C. broadcasts. Beginning with a 1937 programme which concentrated on Yeats, Stephens devoted entire broadcasts to him in 1942, 1943, 1944, 1947, and twice in 1948. Along with many humorous anecdotes, a few concepts dominate these talks. Stephens points out the uniqueness of Yeats's late development and locates his major achievement, as have most later critics, in the verse of the last fifteen years of his life, especially *The Tower*, *The Winding Stair*, and *Last Poems*. Stephens is afraid that too much of the poetry is overly personal: 'Did Yeats too often hang around in his own poems, clank about in his own rhymes? Time will tell' (*JSJ* 92). While admitting that Yeats is 'the "finest" poet of our time' (*JSJ* 97), Stephens wonders if he will join the company of the 'seven great poets' (*JSJ* 94). Finally, Stephens returns over and over again to certain poems: section four of 'Vacillation', 'the most original piece of verse in our time' and 'the highest movement [for 'moment'?] you [Yeats] ever reached in your life' (*JSJ* 66, 72); and 'Sailing to Byzantium' and 'Byzantium', arguing that 'in reality they are only separated in a sense that a preface is separated from its volume, or an overture from its symphony' (*JSJ* 80), calling 'Byzantium' 'the strangest poem' and 'the most remote poem in the language' (*JSJ* 85), and suggesting that Yeats 'had not time to write the third and perfect one' (*JSJ* 85): 'He did not live long enough to compose the third, which would have been the real one' (*JSJ* 100). [59]

In one of these B.B.C. broadcasts Stephens remarked that 'in his later years whenever he came to London he formed a habit of ringing me up and asking me to go and see him' (*JSJ* 68). Thus it comes as no surprise that the penultimate item in Stephens's published writings should be 'W. B. Yeats: A Tribute', written on the occasion of the return of Yeats's body to Ireland and the reinterment at Drumcliff. Stephens's final tribute reads in part:

> There is in his verse much anger, and some peace: much dubiety and some certitude; much of man and woman, and something of God. He liked human beings, without loving them; perhaps he approved of God also without loving Him. He liked ideas better than the things that uphold them. Of love and

passion he preferred the latter : of religion and magic he preferred the latter also. . . .

Was he the greatest poet, and greatest poetic-dramatist in English of our time? I don't know, but he was the greatest poet that Ireland has produced in the English language. He has gone home to his country, and to his deep sleep at last.[60]

*

'James Stephens', Yeats recalled in *Dramatis Personae* (1935), 'has all my admiration to-day.'[61] What Yeats saw in Stephens, I think, was a novelist who had tried to meet the ideals for Irish literature which Yeats had so often enunciated from the very beginning of his career : the use of Irish mythology and folklore in a new imaginative context. As he explained in 1896, 'Emotions which seem vague or extravagant when expressed under the influence of modern literature, cease to be vague and extravagant when associated with ancient legend and mythology, for legend and mythology were born out of man's longing for the mysterious and the infinite.'[62] Thus the association of Stephens with Standish O'Grady, Æ, Lady Gregory, and Synge; and thus his preference for *The Crock of Gold, The Demi-Gods*, and *In the Land of Youth*. That Stephens did not fully attain his goals and that his early promise went largely unfulfilled, I am sure both Yeats and Stephens realized. Stephens never became one of the 'Olympians', never had the honour of seeing his name in a Yeats poem : yet their friendship of some three decades has its place in their careers and in the history of Anglo-Irish literature.

Appendix A : Yeats's Polignac Prize Speech

The text is from Wade 308, *Royal Society of Literature, The Academic Committee : Addresses of Reception* (London : Humphrey Milford/Oxford University Press, 1914), pp. 37–42.

The Blake passage (one of Yeats's favourites) is a slight misquotation from *The Marriage of Heaven and Hell*. The philosopher and statesman Richard Burdon Haldane (1856–1928), first Viscount of Cloan, and the writers and critics Arthur Christopher Benson (1862–1928), Edmund Gosse (1849–1928), and John Henry Newbolt (1862–1938) were all original members of the Academic Committee of the Royal Society of Literature. Examples of the early Stephens poems 'about God and the devil' which Yeats disliked include 'The Whisperer' and 'Where the Demons Grin' from *Insurrections* (Dublin : Maunsel, 1909). 'The sea shall tramp with banners on the shore' is from 'To the Tree' in *The Hill of Vision* (Dublin : Maunsel, 1912); the same volume includes 'A Prelude and A Song' and 'Wind and Tree', the latter quoted in full as the conclusion to the speech.

THE POLIGNAC PRIZE

Mr. W. B. Yeats said : We have awarded to Mr. James Stephens the Polignac prize because of his book, 'The Crock of Gold'. The conditions of the bequest required that the prize should be awarded for some book published in the twelve months that closed with December of last year, and that we should take into consideration the promise of the writer — that is to say, that we should give it rather to a young writer than to an old one. I can only speak of the reasons that made me propose 'The Crock of Gold' and give that book my vote. It has given me more pleasure, I think, than it could give to another man, wise and beautiful though it is, because it is a proof that my native city has begun to live with a deeper life. Mr. James Stephens has passed all his life in Dublin. He has been educated by the literary discussions, by the books and critical standards he has met. No matter how much we seem to create ourselves in solitude, wren or eagle, we proclaim the twigs we have sprung from. I think if he had grown up in Dublin any time before these last twenty years he would have found it hard to escape from rhetoric and insincerity. I hope he will not be offended if I say that even his rich soul might not have saved him from being, like some writers of young Ireland, but a gallant journalist.

During these last years, the Dublin that reads and talks has begun to interest itself in the ancient legends and in the living legends of Connaught and Munster, and here in this book it discovers them weighty with new morals, lofty and airy with philosophy. The town has begun to make, it seems also, in Mr. Stephens' mouth new legends, new beliefs, new folk-lore, and instead of the rhetoric, the hard-driven logic — natural wherever the interest was political — there is a beautiful, wise, wayward phantasy, which an Aran Islander or Blasket Islander would take pleasure in, though not wholly understanding its new meanings, a phantasy that plays with all things, that reverences everything and reverences nothing, an audacious laughter, a whimsical pity. That is the thing I have loved most in Ireland. 'Improvement makes straight roads,' wrote Blake, 'but the crooked roads are roads of genius,' and who would not love that crooked fancy? But until I read this book I had thought the country alone had it, that a townsman had nothing for my love.

Mr. Stephens has made an extravagant language, an extravagant world which enables him to speak and to symbolize his emotions and hidden thoughts, almost as fully as if he were an Elizabethan dramatist with the mediaeval gag but just taken out of his mouth.

We can say so little without an extravagant speech, a vast symbolism. We of the Academic Committee are much wiser than we seem. You will listen to us for an hour, and you will be surprised at how little we shall have said, and even if you do not admire our books very much, you will go away wondering that we could have written them. That is because we (unlike the characters in Mr. Stephens' book, 'The Grey Woman of Dun Gartin' and 'The Thin Woman of Innis McGrath', and the two philosophers, and the God Pan and Aengus Oge) have but our common speech. Mr. Stephens has invented all that phantasmagoria of eloquent people who have an infinite leisure for discussion that he may express the things which Mr. Benson and Mr. Newbolt and Mr. Gosse and Lord Haldane and the rest of us are longing to say but are compelled to keep hidden within us. He is able, having escaped from sobriety and moderation, to express everything : a mischievous candour like that of a school-boy, humour like that of a cattle-drover, a passion for life like that of a girl of sixteen, and the phantasy of a lyric poet.

Our prize is given for general promise and not merely for one book, and that, I think, justifies me in saying that Mr. Stephens had perhaps deserved our award for certain of his poems — for passages in 'A Prelude and a Song,' for instance, had his prose been lacking. When I first met with his name I was not interested; reviewers had quoted violent verses about God and the devil that seemed too easy in their defiance. Besides, I had noticed that when a man of middle life writes his first poem, he invariably writes it about God, for he thinks there is no other subject worthy to occupy the whole of his attention, but I had expected from youth a more original delight. Now I am ashamed that because of these quotations so little characteristic of his rich genius, I permitted others of my country-men to be before me with their praise. I have learned to repeat to myself again and again such lines as that where he describes the sea tramping with banners on the shore, or the little poem which is very simple and very gracious, and not less personal, not less 'crooked' and whimsical because it has inherited a cadence from William Blake.

> "A woman is a branchy tree
> And man a singing wind,
> And from her branches carelessly
> He takes what he can find :
> Then man and wind go far away
> While winter comes with loneliness,
> With cold and rain and slow decay
> On woman and on tree till they
> Droop down unto the ground and be
> A withered woman, a withered tree;
> While wind and man woo undismayed
> Another tree, another maid."

Appendix B: Stephens's uncollected writings on Yeats

The first essay, a review of *Scattering Branches : Tributes to the Memory of W. B. Yeats*, ed. Stephen Gwynn (London : Macmillan, 1940), appeared in *The Spectator* for 12 July 1940. The second essay, written in commemoration of the return of Yeats's body to Ireland, was published in *The Observer* for 19 September 1948; Stephens gives the *Last Poems and Plays* text of 'Imitated from the Japanese'.

HOMAGE TO W. B. YEATS

These tributes to the memory of W. B. Yeats are essays by eight writers who knew him well. There is a preface by Stephen Gwynn, which we could have wished much longer, and in which he might have discussed, compendiously, his reasons for preferring the earlier to the later Yeats. Mr. W. G. Fay's essay, also, is too short. He is the greatest comedy actor that Ireland has produced, and to those who have seen him in his triumphs he is as unforgettable as Yeats himself. He, Yeats and Synge were the Abbey Theatre, and the Abbey Theatre is one complete half of Yeats.

None of the contributors to this book has written at sufficient length, or at sufficient closeness to his subject. They have all, even Lennox Robinson, written of Yeats as at a distance; as if he had not been a companion, a man who lived next door, and whose wife and children and tastes were known to them. And, again, they all write as if they had been more than a little fearful of him when he was alive, and as still somewhat dreadful of his ghost.

At any date of his days Yeats was a remarkable writer, but he was not a great writer until he was practically an elderly man. Then a singular thing, amounting almost to a reincarnation, occurred. It is rare that talent, and its accompanying energy, should mature after the stormy forties of our age, but it has happened. The older Titian was, the greater painter he was. The older Verdi grew, the greater and more exultant musician was he. It was so with some few others, and it was so with Yeats. The older he grew, right to the very day of his death, the better and deeper poet was he becoming, for, where others die finished, he died in becoming, in full flight, and in full fig.

There are a number of Yeatses. There are the poet, the prose-writer, the dramatist, and the critic. In all of these so-varied arts he was curious, and in all but one of them he is to be sought and questioned. I had always mistrusted his prose, as, indeed, I mistrust the prose of nearly every poet. Like theirs, his prose was mannered (mannered prose tries somewhat not to be prose but to be something else), and this prose is elevated on stilts rather than on whatever elevates prose. Once I said to him that he could not tell the truth in prose, but that he could not tell a lie in verse. As to the latter, I do not believe that there has ever lived a soul who has lied in verse. Somehow, by its virtue, its passion, that is, verse will not permit a lie to live (it is possible for a lie to be violent, but not passionate). And also, somehow, by its idiosyncrasy, prose has difficulty in getting truth through — its pace is too languid for the real. There was a something in this great writer, not quite pretence, but neighbouring this, which, as he grew older and greater, he was purging from his work, and from his soul. The desire to be unique and astonishing is one that is natural to every young and talented person; with

Yeats this lasted far too long, nor was he absolutely quit of it at the last, but he was transforming this weakness to an actual vitality, and, had he lived longer, might have made it perform miracles, for his muse was ostrich-like and could digest anything.

As a critic Yeats was exciting and stimulating. He could talk criticism like God or Æ, but when he applied it his criticism went awry. I have rarely known him to praise a particular book, or poem, or picture, without being wrong. But yet, and notwithstanding — which is the oddity — he was a great critic.

There is no space in a rapid reviewing, such as this, to write of Yeats, the dramatist; but here, once again, he is the oddity of our time. There is pure music, pure poetry, but there has never yet been pure drama — Yeats was trying to write 'pure' drama. He is the dramatic genius of our time, as Shaw, moving, singularly enough, towards the same direction, is the greatest dramatist, and both were driving dramatic action from the stage, bringing it to thought, and the word, and betting that the word is greater than all.

JAMES STEPHENS.

W. B. YEATS : A TRIBUTE

*On Friday the remains of W. B. Yeats, brought home
from France, were reburied in County Sligo.*

It is a curious belief of mine (all beliefs are curious, for they all out-run the constable) that a person rarely dies until his or her value has been extracted by his life and his time. Byron, Shelley, Keats all died young. I do not believe that any of these had one single present more to give to poetry. Their work had been abstracted, and all they could have added to it would have been mere recapitulation, and that artistic boredom which is more boring than anything else can be.

Indeed, a commonplace poem (and are there some?) seems to be more tiresome than anything else in life. 'Commonplace' is the wrong word, for what can we love better than it? Air, water, fire; birth and love and service : only the commonplace is lovable, but dull poetry is just dull[,] and is, even singularly, detestable — there are millions of miles of it.

OLDER AND BETTER

Keats might have become a better chemist, he could not have become a better poet. Shelley could have matured into a more diligent husband and father, but not into a greater lyricist. Byron had no more to do in life following the almost immeasurable lot that he had done : he might have been forced to elect to commit suicide 'upon the midnight with no pain'.

Except perhaps in the spiritual life, 'to grow old and bad' is the general physical, intellectual and artistic fact and progress.

But, now and again, miraculously there comes the odd person who seems to grow better in his art as he grows older — Verdi, Beethoven, Titian, Yeats. These, and a few others, seemed to be bettering themselves with age. Yeats died not artistically exhausted. His last volume of verse is not wearisome, and there is in it much to surprise the amateur of his singular art. All that is original is singular. There is in his verse much anger, and some peace : much dubiety, and some certitude : much of man and woman and something of God. He liked human beings, without loving them : perhaps, he approved of God also without loving Him. He liked ideas better than the things that uphold them. Of love and passion he preferred the latter : of religion and magic he preferred the latter also.

If one were asked to name the greatest poetic figures of his time, it could, temporarily, be considered that Gerard Hopkins and W. B. Yeats were the most striking workers that our art has produced. That both of these were 'original' artists, both were oddly self-centred, and perhaps self-deluding, and that both of these had again a dualism or polarity not quite digested into the matter. 'Love's eunuch,' said one, and the other didn't not say it.

One could inquire did they really prefer poetry to syntax, or the other way about. This is a very curious demi-mania[,] and it mainly affects those artists whom we think of as 'classical' : rarely does it obtrude into the work of those whom we think of as 'romantic'. The classicists are almost foreigners to the English language, or are in some sense a little apart, and even a little astray in it. They touch the mind more immediately than they touch the heart.

There are two Yeatses, and to be these the poet had to work like a navvy on a hack. He was a poet, and he was a dramatist. Generally, in lyrical poetry especially, the matter seems to come almost as though it had been 'given'. This was not so with Yeats. He had to work very hard to get his poem. Nearly always he had to write that poem again a few years afterwards : but, finally, he got it. There was a delayed knowledge in his mind. The back of his mind was not satisfied, and it harried him and worried him, so that he had to do it again and again[,] but at the last he got it.

I do not think that he really got his poem 'Byzantium'. He wrote it twice, excellent verse indeed, but I do not believe that, had he lived another 20 years, he would have been able to write it. Away in the back of his head he *knew* of it, but he could not bring it forward. It is strange to recognise a something and thereupon to be unable to express it[.] Milton could not express God the Father or God the Son. These remoted themselves from his mind, as they did from the mind of Hopkins and the mind of Yeats. There is, as Nietzsche says, 'being human, too human'.

EPITAPH

Alas! Towards the end of his life Yeats wrote his own epitaph:—

> *A most astonishing thing —*
> *Seventy years have I lived;*
> *(Hurrah for the flowers of Spring,*
> *For Spring is here again.)*
> *Seventy years have I lived*
> *No ragged beggar-man,*
> *Seventy years have I lived,*
> *Seventy years, man and boy,*
> *And never have I danced for joy.*

Was he the greatest poet, and greatest poetic-dramatist in English of our time? I don't know, but he was the greatest poet that Ireland has produced in the English language. He has gone home to his country, and to his deep sleep at last. Said he to a friend — 'What is the happiest moment of a happy day?' And his friend answered — 'It is the moment when you go to sleep that night, and forget it.'

Appendix C : The respective libraries

The books are listed in chronological order; minor markings have not been indicated. The Stephens volumes are in Yeats's library, now maintained by Miss Anne Yeats in Dalkey, Co. Dublin, or in the Collection of Senator Michael B. Yeats. Through the generosity of Mrs. Iris Wise, the Yeats volumes are now in my own collection.

I. Books by Stephens in Yeats's Library

1. *The Hill of Vision*. Dublin : Maunsel, 1912. Bramsbäck 289.
   In the table of contents Yeats has commented 'lst 5 verses' next to 'A Prelude and A Song' and 'lines 6, 7, 8' next to 'What the Devil Said'. In the text Yeats has marked 'The sea shall tramp with banners on the shore' from 'To the Tree'.
2. *The Demi-Gods*. London : Macmillan, 1914. Bramsbäck 311.
3. *Songs from the Clay*. London : Macmillan, 1915. Bramsbäck 291.
4. *Green Branches*. Dublin and London : Maunsel, 1916. Bramsbäck 293.
   Inscribed 'To W. B. Yeats From James Stephens Oct 16th 1916'. ♯ 100 of 500 copies. Pages 11–18 ('Spring 1916') uncut.
5. *Reincarnations*. London : Macmillan, 1918. Bramsbäck 294.
   Pages are turned down for 'Inis Fál', 'Egan O'Rahilly', and 'Righteous Anger'. One page of the 'Note' is uncut. A second copy of the same edition has all of the note uncut.
6. *Deirdre*. London : Macmillan, 1923. Bramsbäck 315.
   Inscribed 'Hommage from James Stephens to W. B. Yeats'.
7. *Etched in Moonlight*. London : Macmillan, 1928. Bramsbäck 320.
   Inscribed and signed by Stephens — 'To W. B. Yeats : The only things worth reading are "Desire" "Etched in Moonlight" &, perhaps, "Hunger".'
8. *Strict Joy*. London : Macmillan, 1931. Bramsbäck 303.
   Uncut except for 'In Memoriam'.
9. *Collected Poems*. London : Macmillan, 1931. Bramsbäck 298.
   The second reprint of the 1926 edition. Marked in the contents and cut out from the text are the eight poems Yeats included in *The Oxford Book of Modern Verse*; also marked in the contents is 'Anthony O'Daly' and in the text 'On a Lonely Spray'.

Yeats's library also included copies of *The Crock of Gold* (London : Macmillan, 1913; Bramsbäck 309) inscribed 'George Hyde Lees May 1914' and *Kings and the Moon* (London : Macmillan, 1938; Bramsbäck 307) inscribed 'George Yeats 1938'.

II. Books by Yeats in Stephens's Library

1. *A Book of Irish Verse*. London : Methuen, 1895. Wade 225.
2. *Cathleen Ni Houlihan*. London : A. H. Bullen, 1909. Wade 63.
3. *The Pot of Broth*. London : A. H. Bullen, 1911. Wade 61.
   Pages uncut.

4. *The Green Helmet*. Stratford-upon-Avon : Shakespeare Head Press, 1911. Wade 89.
    Pages uncut.

5. *The King's Threshold*. Stratford-upon-Avon : Shakespeare Head Press, 1911. Wade 90.

6. *A Selection from the Poetry of W. B. Yeats*. Leipzig : Bernhard Tauchnitz, 1913. Wade 103.
    Rebound in grey boards.

7. *The Wild Swans at Coole*. Dundrum : Cuala Press, 1917. Wade 118.
    Inscribed 'To James Stephens. With the Kind Regards of Elizabeth C Yeats. Nov. 16[,] 1917'.

8. *The Cutting of an Agate*. London : Macmillan, 1919. Wade 126.

9. *Later Poems*. London : Macmillan, 1922. Wade 134.
    In the table of contents Stephens has marked 'The Song of the Wandering Aengus' and 'A Prayer for my Daughter'. On the back cover he has written the page numbers for 'Red Hanrahan's Song About Ireland' (last stanza marked in text), 'His Dream' ('after running' changed to 'fishes bubbling' in text; the latter phrase was used in former printings), 'The Wild Swans at Coole', and 'A Prayer for my Daughter'.

10. *Autobiographies*. London : Macmillan, 1926. Wade 151.
    On the back flyleaf Stephens has commented 'In this book Yeats is only earnest when speaking of Johnson, & Symons & Dowson etc.' On the back cover he has written the page numbers for the end of section one of 'Ireland after Parnell', the end of section eleven of 'The Tragic Generation', and the latter part of the third paragraph of section eighteen of 'The Tragic Generation'.

11. *The Augustan Books of English Poetry : W. B. Yeats*. London : Ernest Benn, [1927]. Wade 155.

12. *The Tower*. London : Macmillan, 1928. Wade 158.
    On the inside back cover Stephens has listed the page references for various topics, as follows. 'Old age' : 'Sailing to Byzantium', 'The Tower', 'Among School Children' and 'From "Oedipus at Colonus"'. 'Byzantium : 'The Gift of Harun Al-Rashid' and 'All Souls' Night'. 'Pessimism' : 'Nineteen Hundred and Nineteen', 'From "Oedipus at Colonus"' and '"All Souls' Night'. He has also given the page numbers for 'A Prayer for my Son' and 'On a Picture of a Black Centaur by Edmond Dulac' and commented that the former is 'not so good'.

13. *Selected Poems*. London : Macmillan, 1929. Wade 165.
    On the inside back cover Stephens has written the page numbers for 'The Song of Wandering Aengus', 'September 1913' and 'Why Should the Heart Take Fright' (from *The Dreaming of the Bones*). The last poem is also torn out, probably for use in the projected Irish Academy of Letters anthology which Stephens worked on from 1933 to 1935.

14. Oliver Gogarty, *Wild Apples*. Preface by W. B. Yeats. Dublin : Cuala Press, 1930. Wade 279.
    Inscribed from Gogarty to Stephens.

15. Shri Purohit Swami, *An Indian Monk*. Introduction by W. B. Yeats. London : Macmillan, 1932. Wade 281.
    Inscribed from the Swami to Stephens.

16. *The Winding Stair and Other Poems*. London : Macmillan, 1933. Wade 169.
    On the inside back cover Stephens has indicated the page references for the last section of 'A Dialogue of Self and Soul', the second section of 'Blood and the Moon', and section four of 'Vacillation'. 'Byzantium' is heavily marked in the text.
    This copy has an errata slip not noted in Wade, correcting 'yellow' to 'swelling' in 'Old Tom Again' and changing the last line of the 'Notes' from 'She conceived of the Word, and therefore through the ear a star fell and was born' to 'She received the Word through the ear, a star fell and a star was born.'

17. *The Collected Plays*. London : Macmillan, 1934. Wade 177.

18. *A Full Moon in March*. London : Macmillan, 1935. Wade 182.

19. *Selections from the Poems of Dorothy Wellesley*. Introduction by W. B. Yeats. London : Macmillan, 1936. Wade 283.
    Inscribed from Wellesley to William Rothenstein.

20. *The Oxford Book of Modern Verse*. Oxford : Clarendon Press, 1936. Wade 250.
    Advance copy, lacking pp. xlvii–xlviii and the correction slip.

21. *Modern Poetry*. London : British Broadcasting Corporation, 1936. Wade 188.

22. *The Ten Principal Upanishads*. Preface by W. B. Yeats. London : Faber and Faber, 1937. Wade 252.
    Inscribed 'James Stephens from W B Yeats April 19[,] 1937.'

23. *Aphorisms of Yôga by Bhagwān Shree Patanjali*. Done into English from the original in Sanskrit with a commentary by Shree Purohit Swāmi. Introduction by W. B. Yeats. London : Faber and Faber, 1938. Wade 286.
    Dated in three places by Stephens : on front flyleaf, 'June 12th 1938 London'; at the start of the Introduction, 'London June 14. 1938'; and at the end of the Aphorisms, 'London June 1938/Cotswolds Feby 6 1945/London Apl 20 1948.' Various markings throughout the text; drafts of two poems by Stephens on the inside back cover.

24. *Last Poems & Plays*. London: Macmillan, 1940. Wade 203.
    After the text of 'The Chambermaid's Second Song' Stephens has written the following poem :

    > Dull & limp & blind
    > Say you!
    > Never mind,
    > Pay what is due.

At the text of 'Beautiful Lofty Things' he has made the following comment on 'of plaster Saints' : 'The reason the old man was cat-called was that the audience, I among them, misheard the phrase "plaster Saints" as "Blast her Saints". I remember it.' After T. Sturge Moore's note on the dust-jacket Stephens has written 'age 6', apparently in reference to 'that mind which by persistence discerns the truth as William Blake did.' And on the inside back cover Stephens has composed the following poem :

> Alas! So much cogitation!
> Mainly about yourself
> Sometimes about your nation
> And still about yourself.
> Dreaming a passion of dream
> That only was lust in the end[.]

Notes on the text

1 I am most grateful to Miss Anne Yeats and Senator Michael B. Yeats for access to Yeats's library and manuscripts and for their hospitality in Dublin; to the Yeats Estate and A. P. Watt and Son for permission to quote from Yeats's published and unpublished work and to print the full text of his Polignac Prize speech; and to the Oxford University Press also for permission to quote from Yeats's unpublished letters. The full text of the letters (found, unless otherwise noted, in the James Stephens Papers, London) will be included in the forthcoming *Collected Letters*, ed. Eric Domville and John Kelly. I am also grateful to Mrs. Iris Wise for access to Stephens's manuscripts and library and for her hospitality in London; and to Mrs. Wise and The Society of Authors for permission to quote from Stephens's published and unpublished works and to reprint two of his essays.

   Two abbreviations are used throughout this paper. *JSJ* : *James, Seumas & Jacques : Unpublished Writings of James Stephens*, ed. Lloyd Frankenberg (New York : Macmillan, 1964); *LJS* : *Letters of James Stephens*, ed. Richard J. Finneran (London & New York : Macmillan, 1974).

   A portion of this essay was presented at the 1976 meeting of the Modern Language Association of America.

2 *Tribute to Thomas Davis* (1947; rpt. Cork : Cork University Press, 1965), p. 19. For the background to the meeting, see Denis Gwynn's foreword to *Tribute to Thomas Davis*, pp. 5–11; and W. B. Stanford and R. B. McDowell, *Mahaffy : A Biography of an Anglo-Irishman* (London : Routledge & Kegan Paul, 1971), pp. 223–25, esp. the P. L. O'Connor caricature (p. 224). However, Mahaffy's biographers mistakenly assume that the meeting was held on the date originally scheduled (17 November) and are thus led into the further error of remarking that the meeting 'was not reported in the major Dublin newspapers' (p. 225). Nor can they note the irony of Mahaffy receiving 'the King's approval of his appointment as provost' (p. 225) on the very day of the Davis meeting. Yeats's speech was first published in *New Ireland* for 17 July 1915.

3 See especially Æ's long letter to Yeats in December 1905, in *Letters to W. B. Yeats*, ed. Richard J. Finneran, George M. Harper, and William M. Murphy (London : Macmillan, 1977), pp. 151–55.

4 George Moore, *Vale*, The Works of George Moore, Uniform Edition (1933; rpt. London : William Heinemann, 1947), X, 169–70. Stephens was a member of Æ's literary circle by 3 August 1907 (*JSJ* 5–6), so Moore's account must be essentially accurate.

5 In *Jack B. Yeats : A Biography* (London : Routledge & Kegan Paul, 1970), p. 95, Hilary Pyle notes that 'he himself edited and collected, or asked friends to provide poems and ballads which he illustrated.' See also Edward O'Shea, *Yeats as Editor*, New Yeats Papers, XII (Dublin : Dolmen Press, 1975), pp. 48–49.

6 Liam Miller, *The Dun Emer Press, Later the Cuala Press*, New Yeats Papers, VII (Dublin : Dolmen Press, 1973), pp. 38–40. See also *Yeats as Editor*, pp. 48–49.

7 *Memoirs*, ed. Denis Donoghue (London : Macmillan, 1972), entry ♯173, pp. 222–23. ♯171 is dated 27 April at Dunsany Castle; the next date given is 29 April for ♯176. ♯171–74 were probably all written on 27

April, as in ♯174 Yeats remarks 'When I told Lady Gregory yesterday that I was coming here . . .' (p. 224).

8   *Memoirs*, entry ♯170, pp. 221–22 and p. 221, n. 1.

9   *Memoirs*, p. 223, n. 1. Yeats eliminated the sentence on the 'bad poet' when the journal entry was revised for *The Death of Synge* (Dublin : Cuala Press, 1928), p. 26; also *Autobiographies* (London : Macmillan, 1955), p. 519. Cf. Joseph Hone, *W. B. Yeats, 1865–1939*, 2nd ed. (London : Macmillan, 1962), p. 231 : 'He pronounced a hasty judgment, afterwards withdrawn, upon James Stephens, now rising to fame.'

10 *Vale*, pp. 170–71.

11 *Seventy Years : Being the Autobiography of Lady Gregory*, ed. Colin Smythe (Gerrards Cross, Buckinghamshire : Colin Smythe, 1974), pp. 436–37. Stephens had some poems published in *The Nation* (London) for 11 September and 2 October 1909 — his first appearance outside Ireland — so 'Stephen' is surely an error for Stephens.

12 *Dramatis Personae* (Dublin : Cuala Press, 1935), p. 78; *Autobiographies*, p. 450.

13 *The New Age* (London), 11, No. 1 (2 May 1912), pp. 10–11. This review should be added to the listing in K. G. W. Cross and R. T. Dunlop. *A Bibliography of Yeats Criticism, 1887–1965* (London : Macmillan, 1971), p. 33.

14 *The New Age*, 11, No. 2 (9 May 1912), pp. 46–47; *LJS* 30–34.

15 *The Hill of Vision* (Dublin : Maunsel, 1912), p. 73. Stephens's volume and O'Sullivan's *Poems* were both published by Maunsel on 12 March 1912.

16 *Seventy Years*, p. 487. This letter is placed between those of 9 May and 14 May, so we may assume it was written during the intervening days.

17 *The Hill of Vision*, pp. 92–93.

18 In a letter to Lady Gregory on 12 April 1913, in 'Some New Letters from W. B. Yeats to Lady Gregory', ed. Donald T. Torchiana and Glenn O'Malley, *Review of English Literature*, 4, No. 3 (July 1963), p. 31, Yeats notes that 'my French lessons together have taken up all my time since I came here [Dublin].' Stephens was also studying French in the early part of 1913 (see *LJS* 45).

19 From a letter to the novelist Stephen MacKenna on 27 October 1927, in the *Journal and Letters of Stephen MacKenna*, ed. E. R. Dodds (London : Constable, 1936), p. 248.

20 The full text is provided in Appendix A.

21 An interview published under the heading ' "American Literature Still in Victorian Era" — Yeats', *New York Times*, 22 February 1914, Sec. 5, p. 10.

22 *J. B. Yeats : Letters to His Son W. B. Yeats and Others, 1869–1922*, ed. Joseph Hone (New York : E. P. Dutton, 1946), p. 179.

23 See George Mills Harper, ' "A Subject of Investigation" : Miracle at Mirebeau', in *Yeats and the Occult*, ed. George Mills Harper (Toronto : Macmillan of Canada, 1975), pp. 172–89.

24 *Seventy Years*, p. 475. Lady Gregory confuses the titles of two of Anatole France's novels : *Les Dieux ont soif* (1912; trans. 1913 by Alfred Allinson as *The Gods are Athirst*) and *La Révolte des anges* (1914; trans. 1914 by Wilfrid Jackson as *The Revolt of the Angels*). She is also wrong about an 'echo' : *La Révolte* was published on 18 March 1914, *The Demi-Gods*

written in Paris April–June 1914 (*LJS* 132, 134).

See below, p. 17, where fifteen years later Yeats makes the same comparison between Stephens and France in a letter to Olivia Shakespear.

25 Stephens had published 'The Three-Penny Piece' in *The Irish Review*, 3 (September 1913), pp. 334–42, and had also included the story in *Here Are Ladies* (London : Macmillan, 1913), pp. 123–39.

26 *The Letters of W. B. Yeats*, ed. Allan Wade (London : Rupert Hart-Davis, 1954), p. 600.

27 'Literature and Nationality in the Work of James Stephens', *South Atlantic Bulletin*, 40 (1975), 18–25.

28 *Letters of W. B. Yeats*, p. 627; Wade's conjecture is correct.

29 The Berg Collection of the New York Public Library holds a letter from Yeats to Stephens, dated only 'April 2' and written from the Glenmalure Hotel, inviting Stephens and his wife to dinner 'on Wednesday night at 7:30 at the Gresham Hotel'. This letter is listed as item ♯242 in Birgit Bramsbäck's *James Stephens : A Literary and Bibliographical Study*, Uppsala Irish Studies, IV (1959), p. 103, where it is impossibly dated '[1912 or 1913]'. 1918 seems the best conjecture, as it accords with the fact that 2 April was a Tuesday in that year and with Yeats's movements at the time.

30 *Evening Telegraph* (Dublin), 22 May 1918, p. 1. The listing of this item in Allan Wade, *A Bibliography of the Writings of W. B. Yeats*, 3rd ed., rev. Russell K. Alspach (London : Rupert Hart-Davis, 1968), p. 379, overlooks Æ's signature on the letter.

31 Bramsbäck, *James Stephens*, p. 41. See also Hilary Pyle, *James Stephens : His Work and an Account of His Life* (London : Routledge & Kegan Paul, 1965), pp. 94–95.

32 From a letter of 20 January 1919, quoted in Hone, *W. B. Yeats*, p. 316.

33 In *James Stephens*, p. 124, Hilary Pyle asserts that 'The events of the short story "Etched in Moonlight" take place in a dream so that emotions and gestures will be especially significant, for Stephens wished to experiment with the symbolism of Yeats's "system"; the story is a failure, however, because Yeats's system was too complex for him.' But the actual failure is Pyle's, in not knowing that 'Etched in Moonlight' was first published in the *Dublin Magazine* in 1923 (August-October, in parts). That Stephens was little concerned with *A Vision* can be seen in the lack of any correspondence with Yeats about the work, the lack of a single reference to it in Stephens's letters, and the lack of a copy (of either edition) in his library.

34 *Lady Gregory's Journals, 1916–1930*, ed. Lennox Robinson (New York : Macmillan, 1947), p. 268.

35 'Irish Literature Discussed by William Butler Yeats in an Interview by Marguerite Wilkinson', *Touchstone*, 8, No. 2 (November 1920), pp. 85 & 84.

36 *The Trembling of the Veil* (London : T. Werner Laurie, 1922), p. 100; *Autobiographies*, p. 217. Stephens's poem in *Reincarnations* (London : Macmillan, 1918), p. 35, reads 'The periwinkle, and the tough dog fish/ At even-time have got into my dish!' Yeats gives 'The periwinkle and the tough dog-fish/Towards evening time have got into my dish.'

37 'The Child and the State', *The Irish Statesman*, 5 December 1925, p. 393; *Uncollected Prose by W. B. Yeats*, II, ed. John P. Frayne and Colton Johnson (London : Macmillan, 1975), p. 457.

38 See Appendix C for a listing of the respective libraries.

39 *Letters of W. B. Yeats*, pp. 717; 801, n. 1. Wade's note is incorrect in not listing Stephens's name as a Founder Member.

40 *Pages from a Diary Written in Nineteen Hundred and Thirty* (Dublin : Cuala Press), pp. 50, 53; *Explorations*, sel. Mrs. W. B. Yeats (London : Macmillan, 1962), pp. 333, 336 (with capitals on 'Mother Earth').

41 *Letters of W. B. Yeats*, p. 780.

42 In the published version of *A Vision* (London : Macmillan, 1937), this passage would have been the beginning of section XIV of Book IV, 'The Great Year of the Ancients', p. 260. The reference in the typescript to the 'Fourth Book' apparently refers to Book III of the published text (see esp. pp. 222–23).

43 There was a volume entitled *The Thirteen Principal Upanishads*, trans. Robert Ernest Hume (London : Humphrey Milford, 1921), but its length (539 pages) does not accord with Yeats's reference in the *Vision* typescript to a 'little book'. The 1884 volume consisted of 137 pages.

44 'Introduction to "Fighting the Waves",' *Dublin Magazine*, 7, No. 2 (April–June 1932), p. 8; *The Variorum Edition of the Plays of W. B. Yeats*, ed. Russell K. Alspach (New York : Macmillan, 1966), p. 572. Yeats dropped the reference to Stephens when he included the essay in *Wheels and Butterflies* (London : Macmillan, 1934).

45 'Modern Ireland : An Address to American Audiences, 1932–33', ed. Curtis Bradford, in *Irish Renaissance*, ed. Robin Skelton and David R. Clark (Dublin : Dolmen Press, 1965), p. 16.

46 *Modern Poetry* (London : British Broadcasting Corporation, 1936), p. 25; *Essays and Introductions* (New York : Macmillan, 1961), p. 506.

47 Unpublished letter, William Andrews Clark Memorial Library. For a brief account of Yeats's lecture, see Francis Stuart's essay in *The Yeats We Knew*, ed. Francis MacManus (Cork : Mercier Press, 1965), pp. 35–36.

48 *The Oxford Book of Modern Verse, 1892–1935*, chosen by W. B. Yeats (Oxford : Clarendon Press, 1936), pp. 220–23. The other six poems in Yeats's selection are 'Deirdre', 'Blue Blood', 'A Glass of Beer', 'Egan O'Rahilly', 'Inis Fál', and 'In the Night'.

49 *Oxford Book of Modern Verse*, pp. xl–xli, xiv.

50 *Oxford Book of Modern Verse*, p. xli.

51 Hone, *W. B. Yeats*, p. 454; Wade, *Bibliography*, p. 471.

52 Quoted in Hone, *W. B. Yeats*, p. 458.

53 *Essays and Introductions*, p. 515.

54 *The Variorum Edition of the Poems of W. B. Yeats*, ed. Russell K. Alspach (New York : Macmillan, 1957), p. 633.

55 Jon Stallworthy, *Vision and Revision in Yeats's Last Poems* (Oxford : Clarendon Press, 1969), p. 66.

56 *Songs from the Clay* (London : Macmillan, 1915), p. 52.

57 'The Harvest of Poetry : Anthologies Good and Bad', *The Sunday Times* (London), 27 August 1939, p. 4. Stephens is reviewing Robert Lynd's *Modern Poetry*.

58   See Appendix B for the full text.
59   For the full texts see *JSJ* 61–100, which includes 'Some Irish Books I Like'
     (1937), 'W. B. Yeats' (1942), 'Yeats as Dramatist' (1943), 'Byzantium'
     (1944), 'Yeats and Music' (1947), 'Around and About Yeats' (1948), and
     'Yeats the Poet' (1948). In *The Lonely Tower : Studies in the Poetry of
     W. B. Yeats,* 2nd ed. (London : Methuen, 1965), pp. 65, 98, and 109,
     T. R. Henn has taken issue with several of Stephens's comments on Yeats.
60   See Appendix B for the full text.
61   *Dramatis Personae,* p. 78; *Autobiographies,* p. 450.
62   'Miss Fiona Macleod as a Poet', *Bookman,* II (December 1896), p. 92;
     Uncollected Prose by W. B. Yeats, I, ed. John P. Frayne (London : Mac-
     millan, 1970), p. 423.